One North Star

A Counting Book

Phyllis Root

Illustrations by
Beckie Prange
& Betsy Bowen

University of Minnesota Press
Minneapolis · London

Who lives here
under one north star?

One moose browses by a cobble beach
by one great lake
under one north star.

TWO little brown bats hang in a cave
one rough-legged hawk soars
high above the bluffs
under one north star.

Three black bears den
two ruffed grouse roost
one Canada lynx prowls for snowshoe hares
hiding in the north woods
all under one north star.

Four dwarf trout lilies nod
three wild turkeys gobble
two morel mushrooms poke through the duff
one spring peeper shrills *peeppeep peeppeep*
deep in the big woods
under one north star.

Five walleyes fin near wild rice
four blue flag irises flower
three mudpuppies wriggle
two loons call
one porcupine sleeps in a jack pine tree
all along a lake
under one north star.

Six sandhill cranes forage in the grass
five showy lady's slippers bloom in a bunch
four aspen trees quake
three elk graze
two gray wolves watch from a wolf willow thicket
one northern prairie skink basks in the sun
in the aspen parkland
under one north star.

Seven tiger swallowtails puddle
six painted turtles sun
five water striders skitter

four brook trout swim
three otters dive
two bald eagles guard their nest
one hummingbird hovers
by a winding river
all under one north star.

Eight yellow pond lilies float
seven great blue herons cronk
six yellow-headed blackbirds sway
five toads hop
four green darner dragonflies fly
three minks slink
two mallards paddle
one beaver gnaws on a paper birch tree
all in the marsh
under one north star.

Nine mosquitoes whine
eight small cranberries glow
seven red russula mushrooms sprout
six soft-needled tamaracks grow
five cottongrasses puff
four pitcher plants catch flies
three snowshoe hares nibble
two bog lemmings hide
one great gray owl glides
down in the bog
under one north star.

Ten blue-winged teals dabble in a pothole lake
nine showy goldenrods wave
eight milkweed pods spill silky seeds
seven Canada geese honk

six bumblebees buzz
five bottle gentians bloom
four bur oaks rustle
three soldier beetles crawl
two prairie chickens cluck
one red fox trots
across the tallgrass prairie
under one north star.

Who else lives here?

You do.

You live here, too.

With woods and marshes,
bluffs and bogs,
prairie, rivers,
lakes, lakes, lakes . . .

We all live together
under one north star.

NORTH STAR STATE

I live in Minnesota, which is called the North Star State, and this book shows some of the plants and animals I see when I go to the woods and the prairies and the rivers and lakes and bogs. Wherever you live, many plants and animals live there, too. Go outside and look and listen (and count, if you like) to see who else shares the place that you call home.

GREAT LAKE

Along the shore of Lake Superior, the largest Great Lake, you can see ancient lava flows, rugged headlands, and cobble beaches with stones rounded by waves. When the light slants just right, you might see the gleam of Lake Superior agates.

Moose *Alces alces*

Moose are huge: they can grow to be seven and a half feet tall and weigh up to 1,400 pounds. They are great swimmers and can duck underwater for plants to eat. In the winter they eat willow bushes and other woody shrubs.

BLUFFS

Limestone bluffs hide caves, springs, sinkholes, and fossils. Timber rattlesnakes (*Crotalus horridus*) might live there, too, but they are very shy and seldom seen.

Little brown bat *Myotis lucifugus*

In the summer one little brown bat can eat ten mosquitoes a minute. These tiny flying mammals roost in caves and cluster together to hibernate over winter.

Rough-legged hawk *Buteo lagopus*

Rough-legged hawks summer in the arctic and head south for the winter—all the way to Minnesota and other northern states. They are called rough-legged because their legs are feathered all the way to their toes for warmth.

NORTH WOODS

Many trees in the north woods are conifers that hold on to their needles through the long winter. Because northern summers are short, the pine tree needles can begin producing food for the trees as soon as the weather warms in spring.

Black bear *Ursus americanus*

In dens under trees or rocks or dug into the earth, black bears hibernate through the winter without eating or drinking, living off their body fat. (One bear was even spotted hibernating in an eagle's nest.) The females wake for the birth of their cubs, then go back to sleep, waking again to nurse and care for the cubs.

Ruffed grouse *Bonasa umbellus*

In the winter, ruffed grouse grow extra feathers on their shins and extra comb-like bristles on their feet that help them walk on top of the snow. If the snow is deep enough, they may dive or fly into snowbanks to keep warm.

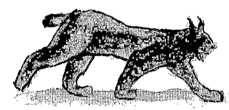

Canada lynx *Lynx canadensis*

Lynx have large furry feet that help them walk on snow. The fur also keeps their feet warm. Lynx eat mostly snowshoe hares, but when they can't find hares lynx eat other small mammals and birds.

BIG WOODS

In remnants of leafy forests, Dutchman's breeches, bloodroot, nodding trillium, and wild ginger flower very early before the trees leaf out and shade the ground. These flowers are called spring ephemerals because they bloom for such a short time.

Dwarf trout lily *Erythronium propullans*

The only place in the world where these endangered dwarf trout lilies grow is Minnesota—and only in three counties. Their leaves are dappled like the scales of a trout.

Wild turkey *Meleagris gallopavo*

Wild turkeys make all sorts of calls, from gobbles to yelps to purrs. They roam in flocks of up to forty birds and roost in trees at night.

Morel mushroom

Morchella esculenta

These spongy, wrinkled mushrooms grow on forest floors, breaking down dead wood that helps nourish the soil.

Spring peeper *Pseudacris crucifer*

Spring peepers are treefrogs that spend the winter partially frozen. When spring comes they fill the woods and ponds with their high-pitched peeps.

LAKE

Thousands of years ago melting glaciers formed many northern lakes. In Minnesota there is even one salt lake, called Salt Lake, which is about one-third as salty as the ocean.

Common loon *Gavia immer*

Loons can dive more than two hundred feet deep and stay underwater for up to five minutes hunting for fish. They carry their babies on their backs to keep them safe from turtles and fish.

Walleye *Sander vitreus*

When they are small, walleyes eat mostly insects, but as they grow they eat minnows and small fish. A reflective layer in their eyes helps them see in dark water.

Mudpuppy *Necturus maculosus*

Mudpuppies are the only salamanders that spend their entire lives in water. The red gills on the outside of their heads let them breathe underwater.

Porcupine *Erethizon dorsatum*

Porcupines move slowly, but their quills protect them from most predators. The quills are actually hollow hairs with sharp barbs. Porcupines don't throw them, but the quills come off easily when touched.

Blue flag iris *Iris versicolor*

Clumps of blue flag irises grow in shallow water and help to protect shorelines. Hummingbirds and butterflies eat the nectar, birds eat the seeds, and muskrats chew on iris roots.

ASPEN PRAIRIE PARKLAND

Where groves of aspen trees, prairie, and marshes mix, they create rich habitats where bison used to roam. Prairie fires kept the aspen trees from taking over the grasslands.

Sandhill crane *Grus canadensis*

Sandhill cranes come to the marshes of the prairie parkland each spring to lay eggs and raise their young. The three-foot-tall cranes bow, leap in the air, and flap their wings in a courting dance.

Showy lady's slipper

Cypripedium reginae

These large pink and white orchids, whose Latin name means "queen's slipper," usually grow in clumps in damp places, even in roadside ditches.

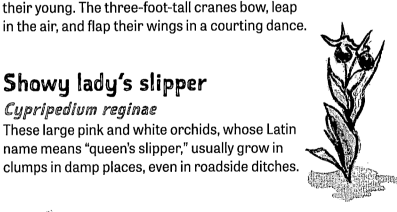

Quaking aspen tree

Populus tremuloides

Quaking aspen leaves tremble in the slightest breeze because their leaf stems are flat and flexible. Their leaves are shiny on top and dull underneath, so when the leaves flutter the trees seem to shimmer.

Elk *Cervus elaphus*

Thousands of elk used to roam the prairie, but hunting and habitat destruction drove them into more mountainous areas. During mating season males bugle loudly to claim territory and attract females.

Gray wolf *Canis lupus*

Wolves live in packs, caring for the pups together. They hunt larger animals like deer, moose, and elk, taking down animals that are old, weak, or vulnerable.

Northern prairie skink

Plestiodon septentrionalis

The body temperature of skinks depends on the temperature around them, so they often bask in the sun to warm up. Skinks can break off their tails if they are threatened. The end of the tail wriggles for a few minutes to fool a predator while the skink escapes.

RIVER

A continental divide crosses Minnesota. Depending on where a drop of rain falls, it might eventually flow in a river north to Hudson Bay; east to Lake Superior and out to the Atlantic Ocean; or south into the Mississippi River to the Gulf of Mexico.

Canadian tiger swallowtail
Papilio canadensis

Swallowtail butterflies spend the winter as chrysalises. When they emerge in the spring they head for wet soil to puddle, sipping up water and minerals from the mud.

Brook trout *Salvelinus fontinalis*

Brook trout live in clear, cool, fast-running streams. They use their tails to sweep out nests in gravel on the streambeds.

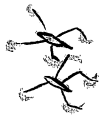

Water strider *Aquarius remigis*

Water striders can skate on the surface of a lake or a river without ever getting wet because they are so light and have claws on their back two sets of legs. They eat insects on the water, including mosquito larvae.

Ruby-throated hummingbird
Archilochus colubris

Hummingbirds are tiny, but they migrate 1,500 miles south each year for the winter, with their wings beating 3,000 times each minute.

Painted turtle *Chrysemys picta*

Painted turtles often bask in a line on a sunny log. They spend the winter buried in the mud at the bottom of rivers, lakes, and ponds.

Bald eagle *Haliaeetus leucocephalus*

When bald eagles are four or five years old, their heads and tails turn white. Bald eagles build enormous nests in trees, sometimes so huge and heavy that the tree falls down.

River otter
Lontra canadensis

Otters often belly-slide down banks of mud or snow. They can hold their breath for several minutes and dive more than forty feet deep. Valves in their ears and nose keep water out when they dive.

MARSH

Most marshes have water all year round and are rich habitats for plants and animals, especially cattails, blackbirds, muskrats, and toads. Some marshes are called duck factories because they are so important to water birds.

Yellow pond lily *Nuphar variegatum*

Water lilies have their roots in the bottoms of lakes and ponds, but air pockets in the stems keep their leaves and flowers floating on top of the water. Water lilies provide food for insects, muskrats, moose, and other animals.

Great blue heron *Ardea herodias*

Herons nest in rookeries of up to one hundred birds. When they wade in muck and mud searching for food, their long, stilt-like legs and thin toes keep them from sinking.

Yellow-headed blackbird
Xanthocephalus xanthocephalus

Yellow-headed blackbirds live in deep-water marshes; red-winged blackbirds prefer shallower marshes. Both kinds of blackbirds need marshes to breed and to feed.

American toad
Anaxyrus americanus

Toads catch insects with their tongues. The eyeballs of toads (and frogs) sink inside their skulls when they eat and help push food down their throats. Each spring a single female toad can lay twenty thousand eggs, which hatch into tadpoles.

Green darner dragonfly
Anax junius

Dragonflies look like flying jewels, but they are fierce predators. They catch insects as they fly, either with their mouths or with their front legs, which scoop insects out of the air.

Mink *Neovison vison*

Mink live near water and eat muskrats, fish, birds, eggs, frogs, crayfish, mice—almost anything they find or catch.

Mallard *Anas platyrhynchos*

Mallards hold their tails up out of the water when they swim so that they can fly straight up in the air if they are threatened. Mallards and Canada geese sometimes nest on muskrat lodges.

Beaver *Castor canadensis*

Beaver use their teeth (which never stop growing) to gnaw down trees for dams, lodges, and food. A beaver's mouth has folds of skin inside that close behind its front teeth and keep water out when the beaver carries a branch in its teeth.

BOG

Peat moss, sometimes many feet deep, makes up the surface of a bog. Underneath is water that is almost as acidic as vinegar. Most plants can't grow in the harsh environment of a bog, and some that do, like pitcher plants, sundews, and bladderworts, catch bugs and digest them.

Mosquito *Culex* spp.

There are many different species of mosquitoes. All lay their eggs in or near water. Birds, bats, spiders, dragonflies, and fish all feast on mosquitoes and their larvae.

Pitcher plant

Sarracenia purpurea

The hairs inside pitcher plant leaves point down, so an insect that crawls into a pitcher plant can't crawl out again. The insect eventually falls into the little pool of rainwater at the bottom of the plant and drowns. Enzymes in the pitcher plant slowly digest the insect.

Small cranberry

Vaccinium oxycoccus

Small cranberry bushes grow along the ground. In the fall birds and other animals eat the bright red berries.

Tamarack *Larix laricina*

Tamarack trees turn golden in the autumn before their needles fall off. They are the only conifers (cone-bearing trees) that lose their needles each year.

Red russula mushroom

Russula emetica

Red russula mushrooms are a sign that fungi are at work underneath the surface of the bog, helping to break down dead plants. These mushrooms are *not* good to eat—their Latin name *emetica* means "producing vomit."

Snowshoe hare

Lepus americanus

In the fall snowshoe hares shed their brown fur, and new fur grows in white. Extra fur grows on their hind feet so they can move on top of the snow without sinking in.

Tussock cottongrass

Eriophorum vaginatum

Cottongrasses grow mainly in bogs. Cottongrass is a sedge, not a grass, and even though its tufts of seed heads resemble puffs of cotton, it isn't related to cotton at all.

Bog lemming

Synaptomys borealis

Tiny bog lemmings are less than five inches long and one inch high. They live in damp places and make round nests lined with grass and leaves underground or in the mossy hummocks of a bog.

Great gray owl *Strix nebulosa*

Great gray owls have wing spans of up to five feet. In winter these owls dive into the snow to capture voles and other rodents that they locate with their acute hearing.

PRAIRIE

Sand prairies and wet prairies, shortgrass and tallgrass prairies—all prairies are seas of grass
and flowers with few or no trees. Less than one percent of our country's original prairies remain in the United
States, making prairie one of the most endangered ecosystems in the world.

Blue-winged teal *Anas discors*

These puddle ducks are dabblers, ducking
underwater in prairie pothole lakes to feed on
plants and aquatic insects. The males have a
white patch on their face and blue wing patches
that can be seen when they fly.

Showy goldenrod
Solidago speciosa

Among many species of goldenrod, this is
one of the most spectacular. It blooms with
tall yellow spikes of flowers in the fall.

Common milkweed
Asclepias syriaca

Milkweed is the only plant on which monarch
butterflies lay their eggs. When the eggs hatch,
the larvae munch the milkweed leaves (the only
food they eat) until they are big enough to change
into butterflies.

Canada goose *Branta canadensis*

Most Canada geese migrate, although some
geese winter on open water. You can hear their
distinctive honks and see them flying in long
V-shaped lines overhead.

Bumblebee *Bombus* spp.

Bumblebees are native bees that nest in cavities,
holes in the ground, or clumps of grass. Only the
queen survives the winter to start a new colony of
bees. Bumblebees are important pollinators.

Bottle gentian
Gentiana andrewsii

The blue flowers of bottle gentians stay so tightly
closed that few insects can get to the pollen
inside. Bumblebees pry into bottle gentians, using
their hind legs to keep the flower open.

Bur oak *Quercus macrocarpa*

The thick, corky bark of bur oaks allows the trees
to withstand prairie fires that often kill other
trees. Because they survive fires, oak trees and
oak savannahs often border prairies.

Goldenrod soldier beetle
Chauliognathus pensylvanicus

Soldier beetles are related to fireflies but don't
produce light. They eat pollen and nectar and help
pollinate plants.

Greater prairie chicken
Tympanuchus cupido

For two months in the spring male
prairie chickens spread their
feathers, leap, charge other
males, and make a hollow
booming call to attract
females on the "booming ground."

Red fox *Vulpes vulpes*

Red foxes eat small animals, as well as fruit, nuts,
and insects. When they have extra food, they hide
it, saving it for when they are hungry.

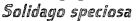

HOW TO FIND THE NORTH STAR

Minnesota is called the North Star State after Polaris, the north star. The earth's axis points directly
at Polaris, so the star stays in the same place in the sky as the earth rotates. If you stood at the north pole
and looked directly overhead, the north star would be right above you.

But you don't have to go to the north pole to see Polaris.

Go outside on a clear night and look up to find the Big Dipper, a group of seven stars that look like a scoop
with a handle. Connect the two stars at the end of the scoop with an imaginary line, and extend this line until you reach
the Little Dipper. The two dippers will face opposite directions from each other.

The line you imagine from the end of the Big Dipper will point to the star at the end of the Little Dipper's handle.
That star is Polaris, the north star, which will always point you toward true north—at least for the next twelve thousand
years. Because the earth's axis wobbles a little, it will point to a new north star in about the year 14,000.

For Robert, who first told me the names of the flowers. —P. R.

For the citizens of Minnesota, who care deeply about their state's arts and natural resources. —B. P.

To awesome Mother Nature. —B. B.

THE UNIVERSITY OF MINNESOTA PRESS GRATEFULLY ACKNOWLEDGES THE GENEROUS ASSISTANCE
PROVIDED FOR THE PUBLICATION OF THIS BOOK BY THE MARGARET W. HARMON FUND.

Beckie Prange's work on *One North Star* was made possible in part by the voters of Minnesota through
a grant from the Arrowhead Regional Arts Council; thanks to appropriations from the McKnight
Foundation and the Minnesota State Legislature's general and arts and cultural heritage funds; and through
a grant from the Donald G. Gardner Humanities Trust in Ely, Minnesota.

Published by the University of Minnesota Press
111 Third Avenue South, Suite 290 / Minneapolis, MN 55401-2520
http://www.upress.umn.edu

ISBN 978-0-8166-5063-7 (hardcover)

A Cataloging-in-Publication record for this book is available from the Library of Congress.

Printed in China
Book design by Brian Donahue / bedesign, inc.

The University of Minnesota is an equal-opportunity educator and employer.

22 21 20 19 18 17 16   10 9 8 7 6 5 4 3 2 1

Phyllis Root loves to muck around outside, in boats or bogs or prairies or woods. She especially loves finding new things she hasn't seen before.

Beckie Prange is happiest getting bug's-eye and bird's-eye views, learning how living things work together, and asking questions.

Betsy Bowen likes it when chickadees come to her window to eat seeds. They talk with her about her art. (OK, not really, not the talking part.)